4400

This book is to be returned on or before the last date stamped below.

5 Oct

385.09   SPENCE,J.

Victorian and Edwardian
railways from old
photographs.

Victorian and Edwardian
RAILWAYS
from old photographs

1   Dowles Bridge on the Tenbury & Bewdley Railway. This
was taken in 1864 at or shortly after the opening of the line
in August. The roofboard on the third carriage, which was
West Midland Railway rolling-stock, reads: "Woofferton,
Tenbury Wells & Bewdley". To add to the mixture, the
engine was Great Western No. 1A, built at Wolverhampton
in 1864 and re-numbered 17 the following year

2   *Overleaf* Railwaymen have always been enthusiastic
gardeners, no doubt often due to the unsociable hours they
have to work. This London, Chatham & Dover porter was
obviously very proud of his marrow!

Victorian and Edwardian

RAILWAYS

from old photographs

Introduction and commentaries by

JEOFFRY SPENCE

B. T. Batsford Ltd
London & Sydney

For Tony Morbin who, at the age of fourteen, lay for many long weeks in Crawley Hospital, and taught us elderly patients how to endure pain and discomfort with cheerfulness.

B. T. Batsford Limited,
4 Fitzhardinge St., London W1A 0AH
and 23 Cross St., Brookvale, N.S.W. 2100, Australia
Photoset by Tradespools Ltd., Frome, Somerset
Printed in Great Britain by
The Anchor Press, Tiptree, Essex
First published in 1975
ISBN 0 7134 3044 3
Text copyright © Jeoffry Spence
Distributed in the United States
by Hippocrene Books

CONTENTS

3 An interesting Edwardian scene on the Caledonian Railway. The location does not appear to be known

Acknowledgement	6
Introduction	7

	ILLUSTRATION NUMBER
Trains and Locomotives	6–32
Stations	33–71
Construction and Destruction	72–93
Rolling Stock	94–97
Signalling	98–101

Staff   102–116

Railway Buses   117–120

Goods   121–126

Hotels & Refreshments   127–133

Steamers   134–138

Royalty   139–142

Notable Occasions   143–155

ACKNOWLEDGEMENT

I am indebted to the British Railways Board for a large number of these photographs which came from some, but certainly not all, of the railway centres to be stored at the Clapham Museum of British Transport, now to be housed in York under the Science Museum; and to Messrs R. C. Cogger, John Edgington, G. Goslin and Geoffrey Holt for much help and advice.

I would also like to thank the following for permission to reproduce photographs: Major Flateau 104; Kodak Museum 71; F. E. J. Burgiss 30; Sutcliffe Gallery 76; London Transport 127; Royal Institution of Cornwall 144. Fig. 139 is reproduced by Gracious Permission of H.M. The Queen, Royal Archives, Windsor and Figs. 4, 7, 16, 25, 34, 47, 61, 62, 66, 110, 115, 130, 137, 140, 149, 151, 154 are from the Publisher's collection.

INTRODUCTION

4 *Fitzwilliam* was photographed at Barnsley in January 1853. It was the engine of the first passenger train owned and run by the South Yorkshire Railway

The railways have always had followers, but in the early days any reproduction of a railway scene had to be done by means of paintings, drawings or lithographs, which historically are not always accurate, particularly in mechanical matters. By the time photography was a reasonable possibility, if only for still life, the railways were well established. Movement was precluded before the early 1870s when Richard Maddox discovered a process that shortened exposure time and allowed moving objects to be photographed.

Unfortunately for us, the photographer of railway scenes has usually shown a disinclination to be interested in human beings. It almost looks as if, in many cases, he evacuated an entire station before he would take his photograph. The railway enthusiast wants his locomotive to be just a locomotive and not cluttered with such distractions as driver and fireman. There must be, or have been, literally hundreds of thousands of photographs of locomotives, taken outside the workshops in all their beautiful, unblemished nudity, and very good photographs they are. But they tell nothing of the social scene.

Historical railway photographs consist largely of two sections: trains and stations. To those whose interest in railways is as general as in many other subjects, one train may look very like another; and a locomotive is something that takes one from A to B, although the locomotive enthusiast cannot really believe that such people can exist and still be happy. Stations are (or perhaps one should say were as standardization has ruined most of them) more scenic, often picturesque, and varied.

It might be thought that with such a large number of photographs as have been taken over the years of trains and stations, signalboxes and construction work, to find 150 would be an easy task in view of some of the known collections in this country. The upsurge in recent years of the publication of railway literature has certainly narrowed the market for original illustrations. A number of those in this book have never been seen before in print, and some of these have not been seen by anybody for a very long time, having been discovered in that great storehouse of nostalgia, the attic.

Official photographs, taken by all railway companies, in spite of their interest to, and value for, the railway historian, tend to lack human interest except, perhaps, for those rather dreadful pictures of members of the staff acting the part of rich passengers looking sophisticated in a new first-class compartment. One cannot really expect otherwise, for the railway company's attitude was, and is, to run for business, not entertainment.

Librarians of local libraries are often historians and take an interest in the history of their district, building up a good selection of local photographic records, including the railway. To examine all the libraries in the country would take up too much of a lifetime, but there must be a great deal of potential material here.

Even nowadays many people are self-conscious when they are being photographed and either look venomous or grin idiotically. One can feel some sympathy for those like the members of the London & North Western Railway Coventry Athletics team (No. 115) who look as if they had to stand with set expressions, and with teeth chattering from the cold, waiting for the exposure period to end. The Great Eastern kitchen car staff (No. 110) on the other hand appear to have been snapped quite casually; probably they were too hard at work to be bothered by photographers. There is always much of interest in the human face: the stiff correctness of the Pullman Car attendant (No. 107), the cheerful joviality of the South Eastern's Inspector taken before 1858 (No. 109), the thoughtful look of the ageing Worthing stationmaster (No. 108). The photograph of the arrival of Sarah Bernhardt at St. Pancras, with retinue, was something of a find. She would be expected to look calm and collected, as befitted a celebrated actress. It must have been a change for her to adopt this sort of pose, instead of one of her outbursts of emotional drama for, as one contemporary report unkindly said, she had become "not so much an exponent of tragedy and comedy as an exploiter of herself", and her style had become "exaggerated and coarse". This does not show amid the noise and smoke of St. Pancras. Apart from the "ghosts" of her prancing dogs, who had obviously refused to obey the order to sit, and a strange floating ghost in the middle, the group of men on her left do not look as if they belonged to the picture at all; rather do they look as if they had dropped straight in from the pub.

One of the irritating things about finding a good photograph is the inability to find out exactly where or what it is, as with the one of the permanent way men at work on the Midland Railway about 1890 (No. 84). The apparent urgency of the work would indicate an emergency of some sort, or why the little group of interested spectators in a lonely country lane? Perhaps it was a Sunday afternoon and they were working off their roast beef; and everyone knows how pleasant it is to watch others hard at work. There is another kind of mystery about old photographs: why a particular photograph was taken. One that was observed but discarded was of a complete London & North Western train of fourteen six-wheeled coaches standing nowhere in particular, with no station or siding in sight. There was one man on the footplate of the engine, probably the fireman, but standing on the track, one hand proudly and possessively on the buffer beam was a portly gentleman dressed in his best suit, hat and frock coat looking as if he had stopped the train specially to have his photograph taken as a memento for his wife. One might wonder on whose authority such a photograph was taken, and it is to be hoped it was only an empty stock train.

Photographs of stations have always been of interest both to the railway enthusiast and the general public. In the early 1900s in particular there were thousands of postcards sold of The Railway Station. It was part of the locality, like the church, the ancient pub and the market place. It was so often the scene of joyful meetings and sorrowful departures. Everybody knew the station and everybody knew and respected the stationmaster. He was an important person in the district who opened carriage doors for first-class passengers, but was equally up to the occasion if young Fred was troublesome and had to be told fiercely to 'op it, quick.

Station architecture varied enormously, depending partly on the ability of the architect, but mainly on the wealth of the particular railway company. Even some of the smaller companies sometimes had very grandiose stations, despite the doubtful expected financial return on traffic, but that often did not bother them: it was one of the Victorian ways of keeping up with the Joneses. Many stations were designed by the companies' own architects, who remain virtually unknown. A few, notably Sir William Tite, were, or became, famous. Tite designed many of the London & South Western stations, including

5   The floods in the West Country in November 1894 created scenes like this one of a train almost trapped at Creech, near Taunton

Nine Elms and Southampton for the original London & Southampton Railway. John Livock designed the Elizabethan manorial stations of the Trent Valley and Blisworth-Peterborough lines. David Mocatta, a pupil of Sir John Soane, was the architect of the stations for the London & Brighton Railway, of which the old Hassock's Gate station is an example (No. 61). One of the neatest of these, Merstham Old station, had the ill-luck to have a bomb on it during the war; it might otherwise have survived as a monument to Mocatta's work.

One station photograph, that of Redhill on the South Eastern in 1865 (No. 64) has been included on the grounds of *un*sociality. The line had been built originally by the Brighton Railway, but when the South Eastern opened its line to Tunbridge in 1842 from this point, the six miles northwards, including the station, was handed over to the South Eastern at cost price, but both companies ran over the same line. The scene at Redhill (as at some other points on the system) was one of seething spite, for the Brighton and South Eastern disliked each other and spent many hours of board-meeting time working out how to do each other down. This lasted until the grouping of the Southern system in 1923, with intermittent rumblings for decades afterwards.

It would be impossible in this Introduction to give a potted history of the railways of Britain, but all lines had their characteristics and idiosyncrasies. The Great Western, even up to nationalization, was always rather superior in its attitude, and let you know it, although third-class passengers were latterly no longer regarded with distaste. Even a train running late always managed to look as if, by some chance, it was meant to be late. The Great Eastern excelled in its dining-car arrangements, a point admitted also about the Midland by those who otherwise made derogatory remarks about it. The London & South Western called itself the Royal Road, and the London & North Western considered it was the Premier Line, an opinion not shared by all its customers, but it was good on punctuality. The South Eastern had a reputation (not entirely deserved) for never running anything at all on time, together with trains of so many different shapes and sizes of rolling stock that they looked rather like the battlements of a castle. The same thing applied to the tough Highland Railway – it had to be tough in view of the weather conditions it sometimes faced; but their late running was always the fault of the connexions with the lines from the south where, in fact, most of the rolling stock came from. The well-known occasion, August 7th, 1888, when the Inverness train left Perth with 37 carriages belonging to ten different companies, was not uncommon at that time of the year. The Great Central was a branch of the Manchester, Sheffield & Lincolnshire Railway. The North Eastern branch lines were known for the paucity of their passenger trains. But they were all real railways with real steam locomotives, and all photogenic. Each company had, and still has, its admirers, even those companies that might be described loosely as the comic turns.

The social pattern in the nineteenth century was altered by railways probably more than by anything else, at any rate for moving about in bulk. In the early days of railways this applied, somewhat naturally, to the richer passenger. The few coppers required for a five-mile journey to the nearest market town was a lot to the poorer class of passenger who might, with luck, be earning ten shillings a week, with a wife and several children to support. (Railway labourers on the permanent way received an average of about 16 shillings a week in the 1860s.) Country people tended to stay where they were, in any case, and if they had to go anywhere at all, within reasonable limits, would walk there and walk back, in the same way that, as children, they had walked several miles to school. This may partly account for the fact that, apart from the staff, the working classes do not appear to have been photographed very much, except for a few well-known and frequently published pictures.

Our railways have a lively and interesting history. It is good to be able to place on record some of the scenes of Victorian and Edwardian travel, particularly as photographs can so easily be lost or destroyed. It would be comforting to think that a proper national collection of photographs of the railway scene might one day be housed in one place.

TRAINS AND LOCOMOTIVES

6 Early days on the Inverness & Aberdeen Junction
Railway, which became part of the Highland Railway in
1865. This locomotive was built as a goods engine by
Hawthorns of Leith in 1858. It was scrapped in 1897

7 London & North Western Railway locomotive No. 402 on a suburban train in the 1860s. Along the roofs of the first class carriages are plenty of pots into which the oil lamps were dropped; the second class got only two per coach

8 Manchester, Sheffield & Lincolnshire Railway: locomotive number 501 designed by Sacré and built at Gorton in 1883. Photographed at Manchester Central

9 The Great Western Railway finally converted its main line from broad to narrow gauge during the weekend 21–22 May 1892. This photograph shows the last broad-gauge train to the west near Teignmouth at 3.15 p.m. on Friday 20th. Half the cross sleepers have already been sawn through to facilitate quick removal.

10 London & South Western Railway locomotive *Tartar*, designed by Joseph Beattie and built by Sharp, Roberts & Co. in May 1852. It lasted until April 1873. One might question the youthfulness of some of the Company's employees

11   The Manchester & Milford Railway, which reached
neither place, was opened 1866–7, with a 41-mile line
between Aberystwyth and Pencader in Carmarthenshire.
Llanybyther Station in the 1890s with an ex-LNWR
locomotive No. 3111 bought by the M & M in 1891; it had
been built at Crewe in 1855 and sold as scrap for £150 in
1900

12 North British Railway Wheatley compound 4–4–0 locomotive No. 224, built at Cowlairs 1871, which was involved in the Tay Bridge disaster of 28 December 1879. It was recovered from the Tay in April 1880 and rebuilt, as a temporary experiment, as a four-cylinder tender compound in 1885. Rebuilt again in 1897, it was broken up in 1919

13 One of the earliest railway photographs: John Chester Craven's locomotive No. 12 at Lovers Walk, Brighton in May 1858. Craven is seated with his family and various employees

14 No. 1 locomotive of the Inverness & Nairn Railway, built in 1855 as a 2–2–2 by Hawthorns, and rebuilt 1869 as a 2–4–0 at a cost of less than £2500. In the cab is William Stroudley, Highland Locomotive Superintendent from 1865 to 1870, when he went in the same capacity to the Brighton Railway. On the tender is Capt. William Fraser-Tytler of Aldourie, one of the Directors

15 Locomotive No. 130 of the London, Chatham & Dover
Railway, built by J. Fowler & Co. 1866 and withdrawn 1908
as South Eastern & Chatham No. 589

16 The Great Eastern Railway at Cambridge about 1860: Sinclair's single locomotive No. 88, as built by Schneider & Co. in 1866, except that it has a Johnson chimney

18 *Below* London & South Western Railway locomotive *Frome*, with 6 ft. 6 in. driving wheels. It was designed by J. V. Gooch, and built by Christie's in 1848. Scrapped 1868

17 *Left* No. 11 locomotive of the Somerset & Dorset Joint Railway was nicknamed *Bluebottle*, because it was at one time the only engine of that company painted blue, which later became the standard colour. It was built in 1861 and exhibited at the Hyde Park Exhibition. It was taken over by the London & South Western Railway about 1871 and worked the Lee-on-the-Solent branch

21 L1 class locomotive of the Great Northern Railway,
built in 1903 and intended for working London suburban
trains over the Widened Lines to Moorgate. It was found to
be too heavy for this section and, although fitted with a
smaller boiler and its water capacity reduced, it was still too
heavy and was withdrawn from the London area. The Great
Northern went in for advertising in a big way at this date,
but it is believed that this locomotive was rigged up with the
advertisements for a special photograph, perhaps for
circulation for management opinion

19 *Left* Great Eastern Railway 4–2–2 No. 609, designed by Massey Bromley and built by Kitsons of Leeds in 1882. There were only a few of this class and the last had gone by 1893, a short life indeed for a locomotive. They had 7 ft. 6 in. driving wheels, which was the largest ever used on the Great Eastern

20 The Colne Valley & Halstead Railway in Essex. The 2–2–2 tank locomotive was built by Sharp Bros. of Manchester in 1849 as a tender engine for the Brighton Railway and converted to a tank engine when sold to the CV & H. This photograph was taken at Halstead

22   Originally captioned as "The Rivals": a Caledonian
large goods locomotive of 900 h.p. and a 16 h.p. car of early
1900s. It was not so many years before the jest about rivalry
became a serious problem for the railways

23 *Above* Stanmore, London & North Western Railway, in 1909, when still rural. The locomotive is a 2–4–0 tank No. 999

24 North London Railway locomotive No. 15A. It was originally one of the London & Birmingham Railway locomotives

25 The Furness Railway's No. 9 locomotive, built by
Fairbairn of Manchester in 1855

27 The Bodmin & Wadebridge Railway, detached from any
other system until 1895 when the London & South Western –
who had owned it (without parliamentary sanction) since 184▌
– joined it to its main line. This photograph was taken in the
early 1900s on the Wenford Bridge branch, which had no
regular passenger service

26 Broad-gauge Great Western train at Marlow, *c.* 1880,
with a 0–4–2 tank locomotive built at Wolverhampton 1868.
It was rebuilt as a side tank in 1884 and not withdrawn until
1935. The Great Marlow Railway was opened 28 June 1873
from Marlow Road station (then re-named Bourne End) and
absorbed by the Great Western in 1897

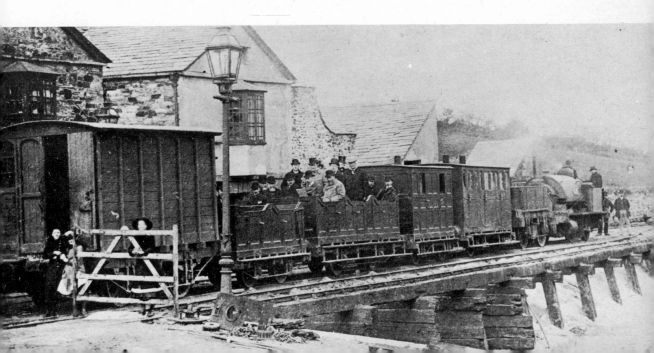

28   The Vale of Rheidol Railway, part of the Cambrian
Railways system, ran from Aberystwyth to Devil's Bridge,
where this photograph was taken about 1902. One of the
most beautiful lines in Wales, it is, fortunately, still open

29   The Snowdon Mountain Railway train at Llanberis in
1908, showing the rack by which the train was run

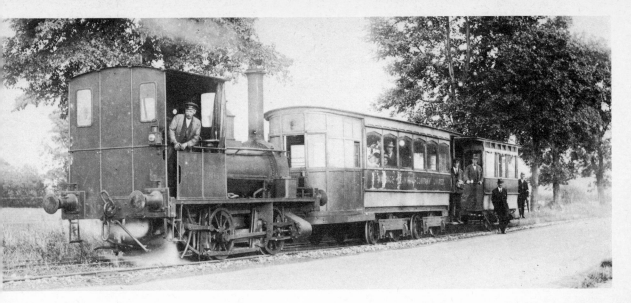

30 *Above* One of England's small railways: the Wantage Tramway in Berkshire, which ran between Wantage Road on the Great Western main line and Wantage Town. It was closed to passengers in 1925

31 Central London No. 19 locomotive was used for the trial trip before the opening in 1900. Locomotives were later withdrawn and replaced by multiple unit trains, owing to excessive vibration to premises above the line

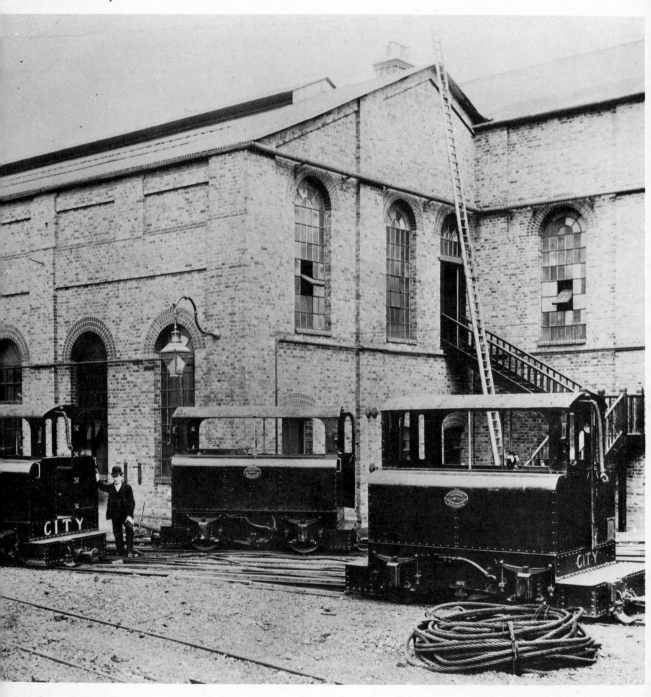

STATIONS

33 Midland Railway: Morecambe Promenade station in 1890. The photographer seems to have commanded everybody's attention, and it looks almost as if the train had been halted specially. The fine roof disappeared with the station re-building of 1907

34 *Above* Bristol in the 1870s. To the right is Brunel's
original Great Western station, and in the centre the Bristol
& Exeter station. The Refreshment Rooms were later removed
to make way for the ''new'' Joint Temple Meads station,
completed 1 January 1878

36 The solid, if rather dull, architecture of Ellesmere
station (built 1864) on the Cambrian Railways, 1895

35   Great Western Saltash station and Brunel's famous
bridge, 1902

37 An early Great Western steam motor car at Halesowen in about 1905. Rail motors were becoming increasingly used at this date, and this was the reason for the opening of many "Halts", a suffix now almost lost

38 Great Western Railway: Acock's Green about 1905, with passengers in a hurry for something. It was not dignified to *run* on Great Western property

40 *Right* Great Western Railway: New Passage and Pier station looking towards Portskewett, and the original route to South Wales until the opening of the Severn Tunnel on 1 December 1886

39 1908: Aylesbury Joint station as originally built. The
Great Western train to Princes Risborough is on the left

41 Platform 6 at Euston in 1908, showing passengers
boarding the 2 p.m. to Glasgow

42 London & North Western Railway's Manchester (Exchange) station, rebuilt 1884, about 1900. There was a connexion with the Lancashire & Yorkshire's Victoria station by a very long platform

43 Rugby "Down" platform in the 'nineties. The carriages, which look as though they might have been uncomfortable, were painted in the London & North Western Railway's "plum-and-spilt-milk" colour

44 Activity at Manchester's London Road (now Piccadilly) station in the early 1900s, when gentlemen wore boaters and ladies' hats were sometimes the size of a hip-bath

46 ✓ *Right* Stranraer: the Town station on the Portpatrick & Wigtownshire Joint Railway, 1900. The original line ran on to Portpatrick, from which point the early steamers to Ireland sailed to Donaghadee, later superseded by the Stranraer–Larne route, the Stranraer Harbour station being about a mile away

45 On the Leeds & Bradford Railway, where they had four classes of tickets: Newlay station about 1860

47 *Right* Some of York station staff in 1909. The two ladies, apparently indifferent to photography, were presumably passengers guarding their luggage!

48 *Above* Chesterfield station, designed by Francis Thompson in gabled Tudor for the North Midland Railway. This photograph was taken 1867–8. The locomotive is a "Jenny Lind" type, originally built at Derby in May 1855 as No. 8. It carried the number 728 from September 1867 to September 1868. After various rebuildings what was left of it was scrapped in 1920

49 *Left* The Lancashire & Yorkshire Railway's special Race Course station entrance at Aintree in 1905. The long wooden platform – which was virtually all there was – was on the embankment on the right. Grand National Day meant a great deal of extra work and extra staff. Trains from many long-distance points followed each other every few minutes, and were run into a huge siding network to await the return journey

50 Winner of the gold medal at the "One and All" Flower Show at Crystal Palace in 1899: Sleights station on the Whitby & Pickering section of the North Eastern Railway. The building, with its mullioned windows, probably dates from about 1847, when locomotives were first used on the line

51 Harwich had for long been an important east coast port, and the Great Eastern opened its branch there in 1854. This photograph was taken a few years later

52 *Right* Redmire, on the North Eastern Railway's Leyburn & Hawes branch which was opened as far as Askrigg on 1 February 1877. The line was closed to passengers in 1954

53 Ardleigh, on the Great Eastern main line between
Colchester and Manningtree. The station was closed in 1967

54 *Above* Cuxton, on the South Eastern's Strood –
Maidstone line in the 1870s. Some of their station houses
were like small manor houses. The engine power is a
Cudworth goods of uncertain vintage

55 Portsmouth Harbour station, for the Isle of Wight ferry,
in the 1870s. It was owned jointly by the Brighton and
South-Western railways

56 *Above* The Lancashire, Derbyshire & East Coast Railway in the 'nineties: Langwith Junction (re-named Shirebrook North in 1924)

57 Port Carlisle, Scottish outpost in England of the North British Railway. The horse-drawn dandy worked the branch until steam was substituted – as late as April 1914!

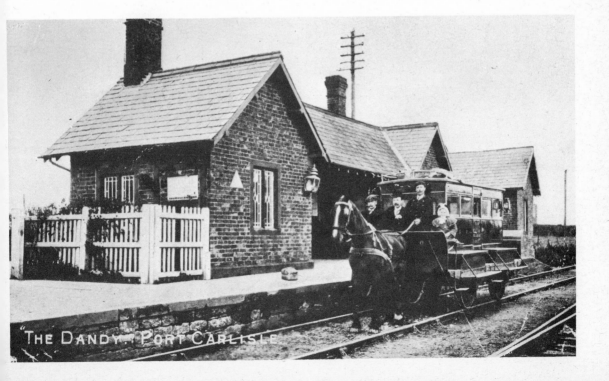

THE DANDY—PORT CARLISLE

58 The old Hayling Island station of the London, Brighton & South Coast Railway, about late 1870s. The locomotive was a 2–4–0 saddle tank built by Sharp, Stewart & Co. in October 1869, was later named *Kemp Town*, and changed again to *Hayling Island* (No. 499) after 1874

59 *Right* The South Eastern station at London Bridge in about 1860, before the extension to Charing Cross was made. It was a hive of activity then as now. The station was designed by Samuel Beazley and replaced the earlier Italianate Joint station with the Brighton Railway in 1851

60 *Right* The Brunel-designed Crediton station of 1854, in about 1895. It was the terminus of the Exeter & Crediton Railway, taken over by the London & South Western after much upset with the Bristol & Exeter. Station horses were held in high regard by the staff, and often appear in photographs of this date, nearly always in a carefree way, blocking the permanent way

61 Hassock's Gate on the Brighton Railway in the 1870s. It is typical of the "roadside" stations designed by David Mocatta for the original London & Brighton Railway. The name was altered to Hassocks from 1 October 1881

62 The London, Chatham & Dover Company's Ramsgate Harbour station, in the early 1900s, conveniently near the beach for its excursion traffic. It was closed in 1926

63 Caterham Old station on the South Eastern Railway, believed to be the day it was closed (31 December 1899) and replaced by the new station (out of the picture to the left, but both old and new signal boxes can be seen). The station, with its steeply pitched roof, was designed by Richard Whittall in "Old English" style, really *cottage orné*. The row of houses (top right) was erected as "temporary" accommodation in 1854 for the men building the line; they were pulled down, with some difficulty, over a hundred years later

54 *Left* Redhill in 1865, looking rather desolate very early in the morning. It belonged to the South Eastern, but the Brighton had running powers through it. The iron pillars were later removed as so many engine crews had their heads lopped off, usually Brighton employees

65 Waterloo, London & South Western Railway, in the early part of the century, and the arrival of one of the more important trains, with furs, feathers, beards and immense portmanteaux

66 *Left* Ventnor, on the Isle of Wight Railway, with its quaintly curved roof. Equally quaint are the doorhandles on the carriages, the doors of which are hinged on the opposite hand

67 The Brighton terminus in the late 1880s, with its massive platform barrier arches surmounted by finials. The new roof of 1883 was the work of H. E. Wallis. One thing that has not changed is the bookstall site

68   A Beattie engine at Eggesford on the South Western's
Barnstaple branch in the 1870s, with mixed broad and
narrow gauge

69 As the Fenland station of Clenchwarton on the Midland & Great Northern Joint Railway was opened in the 1860s, this obviously Edwardian jollification is rather a puzzle, but the cream cake hats suggest a wedding party

70 *Left* The Bookstall at Carlisle Citadel in 1900. The newsvendors appear more interested in the camera than selling to their customers

71 The architecture of Blackfriars, Metropolitan District line station, looks most un-British. Its turrets and moorish minarets and windows were brought down in the London blitz. This photograph, looking rather 1930s, was taken in the 1890s

CONSTRUCTION AND DESTRUCTION

72 An increase in suburban traffic was the reason for doubling the South Eastern's Caterham branch in the late 1890s. It looks very untidy, but no doubt all went well

73 *Opposite* London & North Western Railway: Stockport Viaduct during the widening in 1887–9, when a new viaduct was built on the west side of the original one

74 Heckmondwike cutting, London & North Western Railway, opened in October 1900

75 *Above right* Tunnel construction near Clapham Common in 1898 on the City & South London's tube extension from Stockwell

76 Although ''steam navvies'' were by then in existence, the horse was still the main source of power when the Scarborough & Whitby Railway was under construction, according to the plans of Sir Charles Fox & Son, at a cost of about £27,000 a mile. It took thirteen years to construct and was opened 16 July 1885

77 Erection of a footbridge at Ingatestone on the Great Eastern Railway, *c.* 1900. Presumably the girder remained poised while everyone stopped work to be photographed

78 Opened in January 1863, the Newtown & Machynlleth Railway ran through the solid rock to construct Talerddig Cutting in Montgomeryshire. The N & M amalgamated with a number of other small lines in July 1864 to form the nucleus of the Cambrian Railways

79 *Below right* On 23 March 1895 the sandy soil above St. Katherine's Tunnel (properly known as Sand Tunnel), south of Guildford, subsided and completely blocked the line for several days, preventing South Eastern trains going to Reading and South Western trains going to Portsmouth. Beyond can be seen the entrance to Chalk Tunnel

80 Crewe station and improvements to the goods lines in the early 1900s. The view is looking north. Most buildings and the Spider Bridge have now gone

81 Construction of a bridge at Cleeve, Gloucestershire, on the Midland Railway in 1884

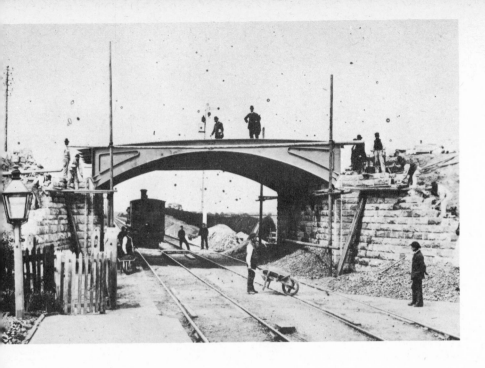

2 *Below* Work on the South Eastern & Chatham near
borough Market Junction early this century. The view is
from Cannon Street Bridge

83 *Above* South Eastern & Chatham Railway: Sundridge New Cutting in 1902. This earthwork was on the south of the new Chislehurst Tunnel during quadrupling of the line t[o] Orpington

84 *Left* This is a permanent way gang on the Midland Railway dated about 1890, but the actual whereabouts do not appear to have been recorded

85 London & North Western Railway: Lime Street Tunnel, outside Liverpool. The quadrupling of the lines between Edge Hill and Lime Street was completed in June 1885. Whe[n] the lines were being made, the tunnel itself was opened out at various points, and it became unnecessary to provide lamps in each compartment when trains entered and left Lime Street station

86 Midland Railway: demolishing Sinfin Bridge, near
Repton, Derbyshire, 1895

88 *Right* Llandulas Viaduct, on the Chester & Holyhead
line, was washed away during a heavy storm on 17 August
1879. The new viaduct was opened 28 days after the
washout, during which period a temporary bridge and line
had been made. Electric light was used for the first time on
the railway to enable work to be carried out at night

37 *Above* The high chalk cliffs between Folkestone and
Dover have several times shed themselves on to the South
Eastern main line below. One such landslip occurred on 12
January 1877 and the photograph shows the official
reopening in the following March. Sir Edward Watkin, the
Chairman, is the figure in the cossack-type hat. The
locomotive is Cudworth's 2–4–0 class E, fitted with stovepipe
chimney

89 *Above* The London & North Western accident at Shrewsbury in October 1907. This was the third (and, fortunately, last) runaway accident in just over a year – Salisbury and Grantham were the previous ones – and the public were getting alarmed. They all happened to night expresses on a curve and in all cases the engine crews were killed

90 *Above* Cleaning up the débris after the derailment at
Stoat's Nest on the Brighton line on 29 January 1910. It was
due to a wheel shifting on its axle, causing a coach to mount
the platform, where it overturned, killing several
passengers and persons on the platform. The odd name of
Stoat's Nest (a nearby farm) filled some nervous passengers
with foreboding and the name was changed to Coulsdon &
Smitham Downs

91 The effect caused by a Kirtley 0–6–0 locomotive
charging the Midland Railway's signal box at Wymondham
Junction, near Melton Mowbray on 3 December 1892

92 *Above* The Midland Railway accident at Amberswood on 24 July 1900. Considering most of the train was derailed and thrown down an embankment, only one person was killed. An artist nonchalantly makes a sketch

93 *Below* London, Chatham & Dover Railway locomotive *Phyllis* which somehow managed to land on two trucks of coal after a collision at Longhedge in 1876

94   Aberdeenshire Railway 3-compartment carriage of 1848 photographed in 1907, showing the luggage rack on the roof and the guard's outside seat which he used, presumably with some discomfort, in all weathers. The carriage was preserved by the Caledonian Railway

95 1st class rolling stock for the Brighton Company's
Newhaven Boat trains in 1908

96 *Right* A compartment in one of the London & South Western Railway's "Eagle" sleeping cars of 1907–8, built for the Plymouth boat trains.

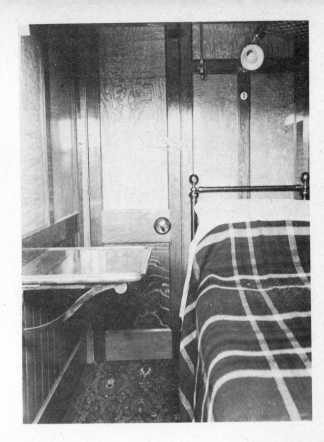

97 *Below* Caledonian Railway invalid carriage built at St. Rollox in 1890. This was a good way to travel if you had the money

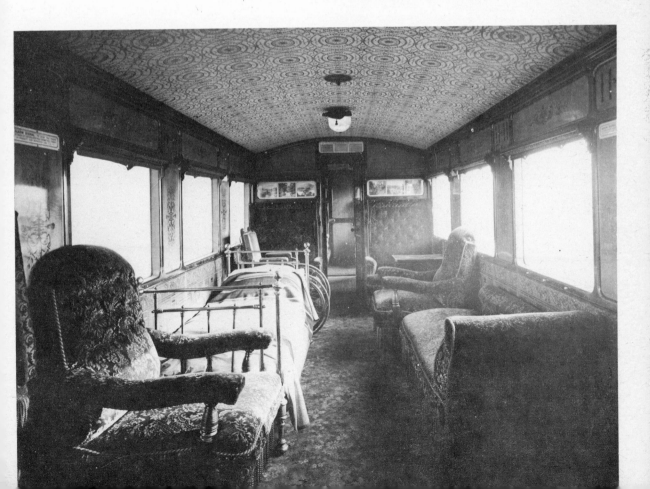

SIGNALLING

98 Waterloo "A" Signal Box 1905–10. It was erected in 1892

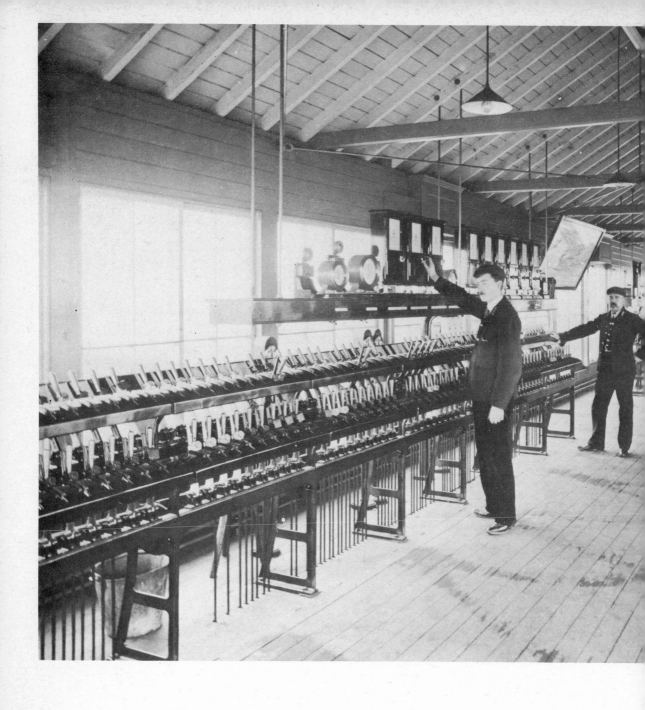

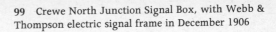

99 Crewe North Junction Signal Box, with Webb & Thompson electric signal frame in December 1906

100 Midsomer Norton Signal Box on the Somerset & Dorset Joint Railway, 1902. The signalman grew a rose tree round his box and up the adjoining telegraph pole and sold the rosebuds in aid of Bath Hospital

101   Littlehampton Signal Box in June 1886. Many of the
Brighton Company's boxes were of this pattern. They
favoured weather-boarding on stations and boxes

102 Porter W. Kidd of Cambridge, Great Eastern Railway in 1876. He retired as driver at Stratford in November 1920 and died, aged 90, in 1945. The photograph had been coloured, the cap and jacket being olive green, a colour believed to have been used by the earlier Eastern Counties Railway. The tie was a light Cambridge blue, but this may have been his own choice

103 Some London, Brighton & South Coast Railway wages staff in 1881. From left to right: ticket collector, ticket inspector, station superintendent, station inspector, guard, policeman

104 Showing pride in his craft: a South Eastern signalman of about the 1860s, with his model signals

105 *Above* Station staff, believed to be at Lewisham, in the 1890s. It is not often that one sees a photograph with passengers actually in a compartment

106 *Left* London & North Western Railway guard and porters loading up at Euston in 1906

108 Alfred Thomas Chapman, stationmaster at Worthing, who held the position for 40 of his 47 years' service from 1860 to 1907

107 Pullman car attendant of 1910. They always wore a distinctive uniform

109 An early photograph of a railway uniform: Thomas Hamerton, Inspector on the South Eastern Railway, who died in 1858

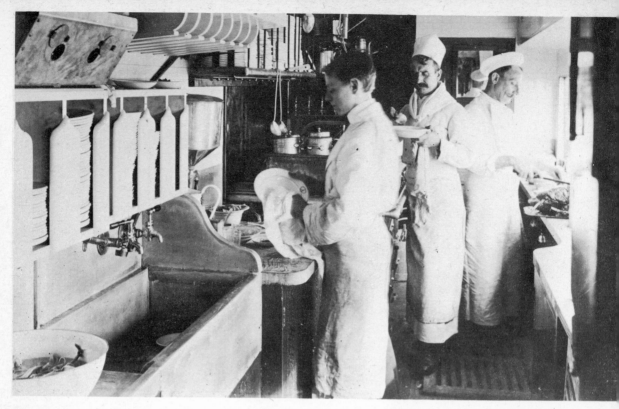

110 *Above* Great Eastern Railway kitchen car staff of the Norfolk Coast Express in 1907. In each of these cars a table d'hôte lunch and dinner could be cooked for 130 passengers

111 *Below* Old stagers: staff of the Midland Railway's Locomotive Department at Derby about 1860, grouped in front of a Kirtley 0–6–0 goods tender locomotive

Breakfast on the Great Central Railway. Navvies at
gham, 1896, when the London extension was being

113 Carlisle Citadel station staff about 1890. Carlisle was
worked by the Citadel Station Committee, but trains of the
LNWR, Caledonian, Midland, North British, North Eastern,
Maryport & Carlisle and Glasgow & South Western used the
station. A very mixed staff was photographed here

114 A stationmaster on the London & North Western was not averse to giving the ''right away'' signal himself in 1905

115   Even in 1910 the strain of being photographed was reflected in the self-conscious expressions of the London & North Western Coventry Athletics team. Shorts were apparently worn long that year

116   Edward Entwistle, born 1815, was fireman on the *Rocket* from 1831 to 1833, and died in 1909. This photograph was taken in 1905

RAILWAY BUSES

117   The Great Western Railway started "Sightseeing Cars"
about 1907. This one is about to leave Paddington on a tour
of London

118 Inter-station horse buses were a regular feature of
London's transport early this century. This is a London &
North Western bus to Charing Cross outside the Euston
Hotel about 1905

119 By 1904 the railways were engaged in running their
own feeder bus services. Here is a Durkopp Omnibus of the
North Eastern Railway, used on the Beverley to Driffield
service

120 Charabancs, too, were used by some of the railways:
Hallford charabanc of the North Eastern preparing to leave
from the *Black Swan* at Kirby Moorside. One might question
the comfort of such a pleasure trip, with solid tyres on roads
of poor surface, exposed to all weathers

121   Loading rabbit traffic at North Tawton, on the northern fringe of Dartmoor, 1906. Many stations in the south west dealt with this traffic, a large proportion going to Birmingham. Most farmers employed trappers for the season, remuneration being board and lodging and 1d. or 1½d. for each rabbit caught

122 In 1900 the four big breweries of Worthington, Bass, Samuel Allsopp, and Ind Coope all had private railways at Burton-on-Trent, connecting with the main lines. This Worthington beer train was drawn by one of the firm's private locomotives

123 Express Parcels delivery van of the North Eastern Railway, early 1900s

124 Great Western Railway 2-ton goods lorry 1905, conveying W.D. & H.O. Wills's tobacco traffic

126 The principal goods station of the Caledonian Railway at Buchanan Street, Glasgow, first opened in 1850. At the date of this photograph – about 1906 – 48,000 packages a day were passing through the station by 1000 wagons and 800 lorries each way.

25   A once familiar sight (and sound) on railway stations,
his shows the milk dock at Euston in 1902, where 5000
hurns were dealt with daily at this date

127 Charing Cross Hotel and a crowded Strand in 1888. The Metropolitan Railway ran the "Umbrella" buses

128 The Coffee Room of the Midland Railway St. Pancras Hotel in June 1876

129 *Right* Euston tea trolley service about 1908. The menu does not look very exciting, but at least there were plenty of staff to deal with it

130 *Below* 3rd class dining car on the Great Northern Railway about 1900. Dinner was described as "good, cheap and well-served". A bottle of champagne was 8s. to 10s.

131 The Euston Hotel in 1896. Before the centre block was built, the buildings on the left and right were the original Euston and the Victoria Hotels. The architect of the two older hotels was Philip Hardwick, who had designed the Doric Arch or Portico. The later hotel dated from 1880–1, and was designed by J. B. Stansby, the Company's architect. It blocked the view of the Portico which was no longer the "Gateway to the North"

132 June 1896: perched on a hill overlooking Avenham Park and the Ribble Valley, the Park Hotel at Preston, with its turrets and tall chimney stacks, rather resembles a sort of Dracula mansion in a horror film. Designed by Arnold Mitchell and opened in 1882, it was owned jointly by the London & North Western and Lancashire & Yorkshire Railways. It remained in railway hands until after nationalization

133 A corner of a London & North Western 1st class dining saloon in September 1898. The postal box was an added convenience

134 Part of Southampton Docks in the 1870s. Even at that date the docks covered quite a large area

136 *Below* Holyhead Harbour with London & North
Western boats for the crossing to Ireland. Taken from the
Station Hotel on 21 September 1905

135 Paddle steamer *Brittany* at St. Peter Port. One of the
London & South Western fleet, it was built in 1864 and sold
in 1900

137 *Below* Greenock, Princes Pier, with P.S. *Neptune*, built
1892 for the Glasgow & South Western Railway by Napiers.
It was sunk in April 1917 as H.M.S. *Nepaulin*

138 The S.S. *Oceanic* at Liverpool Landing Stage 10 August
1904. The London & North Western made connexions with
transatlantic steamers over the Mersey Docks Lines. To the
left is the Riverside Station

139   Great Eastern Royal train from Wolferton to Sheffield
26 April 1909, showing the Prince and Princess of Wales
(later King George V and Queen Mary)

140 The Great Western Royal train from Windsor to Folkestone near St. Mary Cray on the London, Chatham & Dover on 11 March 1899

142 *Below* King Edward VII's journey from Ollerton (near where he was staying) to Doncaster Races in September 1906 was made in the London & North Western's Royal train, although Ollerton was a Lancashire, Derbyshire & East Coast Company's station, and the locomotive was LD & EC 0–6–2 built by Kitsons of Leeds

141 David Hughes, M.V.O. Great Western Royal train driver from 1889 to 1901

143 Decorating locomotives for special occasions was very much the thing in late Victorian and Edwardian times. This is a London & South Western Drummond T9 No. 120, photographed in connexion with a Boer War special train for General Sir Redvers Buller

145   1908. Arrival of a special football excursion at Park
Royal, which the Great Western Railway had built as an
encouragement to the game. The crowd does not look as if it
is armed with knives and hammers to wreck the train on the
return journey. *O Tempora! O Mores!*

144 Padstow, awaiting the arrival of the first passenger train on 27 March 1899

146 *Below* Widney Manor station, near Solihull in Warwickshire. The Great Western opened the station on 1 July 1899, following a covenant between the railway and the Greswolde family in 1897 to maintain a station for 15 years, and to run not less than six stopping passenger and one stopping goods train each day of the week. It somehow escaped the eagle eye of Dr. Beeching and has managed to survive

147 *Above* Cutting the first sod of the Metropolitan Extension at Aylesbury on 10 May 1890. This had always been an occasion for a ''cold collation'' and general flag-waving

148 The festive opening of the Great Central to London at Marylebone on 9 March 1899. The train, drawn by locomotive No. 861, was despatched by the Rt. Hon. C. T. Ritchie, President of the Board of Trade. Public service started on 15 March

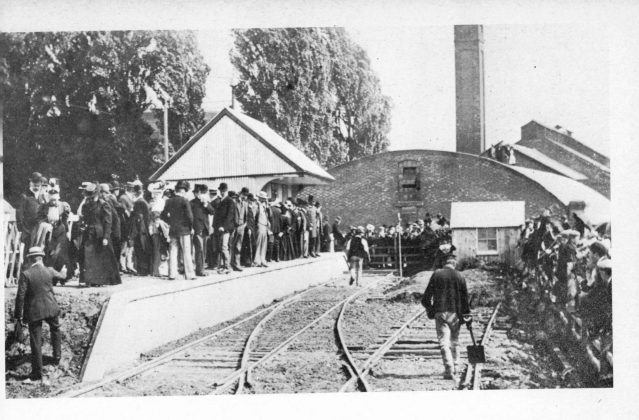

149 *Above* The crowd at Chichester on 27 August 1897 awaiting the opening of the Hundred of Manhood & Selsey Tramway (West Sussex Railway). The line was closed to passengers on 19 January 1935

150 The Hereford, Ross & Gloucester branch of the Great Western was originally broad gauge, and this photograph shows the narrowing completed in August 1869

151 The two-day railway strike, 18–19 August 1911, made it necessary to bring out the army to guard vital points, of which the Brighton Company's Clapham Junction North Signal Box was apparently one

2 *Left* London & North Western rail motor at Dyserth in
05. This may have been an inauguration ceremony of the
w service with a well-heeled crowd of officials, the two
ting presumably being VIPs

53 *Left* The first train to arrive at the Hope Mill terminus
f the Cranbrook & Paddock Wood Railway on 12
eptember 1892. Locomotive No. 112 was designed by
udworth in 1863, and withdrawn 1901. Hope Mill was
enamed Goudhurst on 1 December 1892

154 Off for the August Holidays! At Paddington in the
early 1900s, when passengers took a great deal of luggage.
This group looks bored, so perhaps the train was late getting
in to the platform. Surely it couldn't have been a
cancellation?

155 Arrival at St. Pancras of the great French actress, Sarah Bernhardt on 28 July 1894. The special Midland saloon in which she had travelled had a communication cord which hung outside the carriage